PRACTICAL HOME RESTORATION

CANING

— • AND • —

RUSHWORK

PRACTICAL HOME RESTORATION

CANING

· AND ·

RUSHWORK

YVONNE REES

WARD LOCK

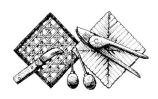

ACKNOWLEDGEMENTS

With thanks to the Wycombe Cane and Rush Centre for their professional help in preparing the text and pictures for this book and to the High Wycombe Chair Museum for allowing us to photograph some of their wonderful chairs.

Colour photography: Chris Challis

A WARD LOCK BOOK

First paperback edition 1995
First published in the UK 1993
by Ward Lock, Wellington House, 125 Strand,
LONDON, WC2R 0BB

An imprint of the Cassell Group
Copyright © Yvonne Rees 1993, 1995

Distribution in the United States
by Sterling Publishing Co., Inc.
387 Park Avenue South
New York
NY 10016-8810

Distribution in Australia
by Capricorn Link (Australia) Pty Ltd
2/13 Carrington Road, Castle Hill NSW 2154

A British Library Cataloguing in Publication Data block for this book may
be obtained from the British Library

ISBN 0-7063-7445-2

Printed and bound in Spain by
Graficas Reunidas, Madrid

CONTENTS

INTRODUCTION

*T*here is something immensely satisfying in taking what looks to be little more than a bundle of grass or twigs and transforming it into a large three-dimensional object with a real practical use such as a chair or basket. As in all ancient crafts – and this one dates back at least 4000 years to the Ancient Egyptians – the raw materials are relatively humble and easy to obtain, no real specialist tools are needed and the end product is a functional everyday item that can be as simple or ornate as time and talent permit.

Handmade baskets are not merely functional, they can make the most beautiful accessories too. A little roughness or naivety in their construction usually only adds to their charm. Mastering even the most basic techniques will give you the ability to use different colours, shapes and patterns to create receptacles for dried flowers, magazines, a collection of fir cones, fruit and vegetables or kitchen utensils. These can be placed on the floor or a table, be hung from the ceiling on butcher's hooks, or fastened to the wall.

There is a wide choice of traditional designs – and purposes – from the shallow wide–bottomed basket, principally developed for gathering fresh herbs, to the close-woven egg basket. Look out for different baskets on antique stalls and in rural or lifestyle museums; remarkably many have only the attractive patina of age as evidence of centuries' use. You can often spot interesting baskets in old paintings and engravings too.

Chair mending in 1795 – a craft that has remained the same to the present day. (Mary Evans Picture Library)

INTRODUCTION

INTRODUCTION

If you fancy trying the craft yourself, the old-fashioned styles are quite easily copied; or you might prefer to adapt the traditional techniques to a few ideas of your own. Alternatively, you may be interested in learning basket-making in order to repair a well-loved but damaged basket, or a charming junk shop bargain: an old picnic hamper perhaps, or a classic fruit picker. Repairs can usually be made to look fairly authentic by choosing your materials carefully and staining or dyeing them to match the original.

Repair and restoration are also often the main motivations for wanting to learn the kind of caning and rushwork techniques so popular in the last couple of centuries, for making simple country chairs marginally more comfortable. Thousands of these sturdy wooden chairs were produced – and carts used to leave the chair-making centres piled impossibly high with them.

Since a great many of the chairs were intended for communal use – in a church or village hall – the seats of those you can pick up today in auction sales and antique shops are often damaged, with the cane or rush ripped and hanging down, or maybe only a few shreds remaining. Usually the sturdy chair frames survive and the seats are easily restored if you have the patience and inclination to learn the craft. Such chairs may be quite plain although some are more decorative in a solid, dignified way. Any could look splendid re-seated, especially in country-style interiors; in sets they make excellent dining chairs around a plain wooden table or trestle. Single chairs may be just right for a bedroom, bathroom or hallway.

Whether working in cane, rush or willow, you will not find the basic techniques difficult once you have mastered handling the material. You will need plenty of floor space so try to have an empty room or yard to work in; patience is soon lost when bumping elbows or tangling with other items! If you are a beginner, it is sensible to make a modest start – don't over-reach yourself by taking on too large or complicated a project. If you start with something simple – perhaps even tackle some sample stages until you become more confident –

INTRODUCTION

you will soon build up your proficiency.

If you would just like someone looking over your shoulder in the early stages, there are plenty of day and weekend courses which can be great fun and usually ensure you come home with something to be proud of and plenty of enthusiasm for continuing the craft. Check your local adult education classes or contact your national craft association.

One advantage is that you do not need large or expensive specialist equipment for any of these crafts; in fact many can be improvised (page 19). However, buying the materials is frequently not such an easy matter. Specialist suppliers tend to deal only with tutors or other professionals and will only sell in large quantities – far more than you can justify buying. You can either get supplies through your tutor if you have one, or club together with fellow enthusiasts to make a bigger order; some growers and importers will accept smaller orders providing you collect the goods yourself – which is all right if you live within a reasonable distance. Once you have found a supplier for your raw materials, do make sure you have somewhere suitable to store them – the warm, dry atmosphere of a house is no good at all – and remember bundles of cane or willow are long and bulky.

STYLE GUIDE

*O*ne of the very first crafts developed by man was the weaving, plaiting and winding of long, strong flexible vegetable material to make sturdy objects for practical everyday use. The material which was used usually depended on whatever was readily available locally. In colder climates this would mean willow, split wood, rush, roots, bark and grasses. In warmer ones, bamboo, cane, palm leaf and fibre were used – as indeed they still are.

The African and Eastern tradition of round baskets set on a square base, incorporating glossy patterns of red, black and natural cane, has been passed down through countless generations. China, Japan, Malaya and Borneo developed their own style of split bamboo baskets – the better sort using pegs rather than nails. Palm leaf has always been favoured in the East Indies as a basket-making material – particularly the screw palm which splits easily, although raffia palm and Buris palm are also used. In earliest times, these would be cut with sharp stones or broken shells, with a pointed bone making a handy bodkin to complete this most primitive set of tools.

Cane and later pulp cane – the rounded cut centre of the cane – was particularly prized where it was readily available. It is pliable when damp, can be cut in good lengths for working and is easier to use than willow. Yet canework can be sturdy enough to make large pieces of furniture.

Despite its evident popularity and traditional usage, cane is a relatively recent introduction to Northern Europe, where willow is abundant and has always been the dominant basket-making material. Even so, most of England's willows were imported from the major

STYLE GUIDE

growing areas of Belgium, France, Germany and Madeira; it is only since 1914 that the home-grown centres on the Somerset levels, and in the Thames and Trent valleys, have been developed.

Such materials might be used to make anything from a coffin to fish and animal traps, wattle fences, coracle boats or even a hut. Water and food were once heated in clay-covered baskets which could safely be put on the fire – from at least since 8000 BC, if Greek and Bronze Age archaeological evidence is to be believed.

What is surprising are the similarities between the construction and appearance of objects separated by thousands of miles or years. Central and West African baskets are the same today as they were many centuries ago. Equally the numerous examples of Egyptian woven work from around 3000 BC, which have been excavated, including sandals and furniture – usually reserved for the Pharaoh – display a tradition of coiled work that can still be found in most ethnic communities.

Early North European basketwork, on the other hand, tends to use the principle of a slath base – interlocked sticks with the material woven around strong upright stakes. India's bitumen-covered basket boats are almost identical to the fifth-century BC remains found in the Euphrates, or even Britain's ancient skin-covered coracles. Basketwork seems to have served every purpose through the ages. There have been light but strong carts, balloonists' baskets and even basketwork shell cases which were used by Charles II's army.

From the very earliest baskets and other canework man has explored the possibilities of decorative design by including ceremonial symbols (in India), plaiting and coiling the material (in Ancient Egyptian sandals) or incorporating other materials to produce a variety of colours and patterns. Grasses, palm, corn leaves, rushes, hemp, aloe, yucca, willow and the roots of cedar, spruce and alder have all been used, sometimes dyed brown, red, black or yellow with natural plant dyes. Yucca, for example, produces a strong red dye from the roots and a yellow one from the leaves.

SECTION ONE

Often the colours have had a particular religious or ritual significance: in India red was sacred and represented the east and success, blue stood for the north symbolizing defeat and trouble, black for the west and death, while white represented peace and happiness. Patterns incorporated in the design were significant too. You might find suns, moons, stars, animals, plants, clouds, trees, weapons, dancing, birds, or even the movement of water – to convey some message.

Basket-making may probably be our most ancient craft, but it is one that has not as yet been successfully replaced by any mechanized method – even mass-produced imports are handmade. Originally any pliable material was used to make containers for carrying or storing virtually anything – wood, vines, leaves, grasses or any fibrous matter would all be pressed into service. Gradually, oak, ash and hickory splints were replaced by flat reeds, while oak, willow and other vine-like materials useful for twined or ribbed baskets have been replaced by round reeds. Pollarding techniques were developed by the earliest settlements ensuring that the raw materials were always plentiful. Then someone had the bright idea of pressing clay around the baskets to take their shape and thus clay pots were born.

Baskets, however, continued to be the practical alternative for other uses. Like patchwork quilt patterns and some old country chair styles, many basket types have special traditional names – these may have developed from their use, their shape, their maker or the place where they were made. Thus the Williamsburg basket is a shape popularized in that district of the United States; the traditional herb basket is shallow and flat bottomed; the Nantucket Lightship basket from Massachusetts, woven over a wooden mould, was originally made almost exclusively on Nantucket Island. Many of the old words used to describe a particular type of basket are being lost from the language: the English Shropshire whisket, the maund or fish basket, the seaside groins made of hazel called radlings on the north-west coast of England.

STYLE GUIDE

Tracing the development and style of working baskets across the world can be a fascinating study. Those French willow eel traps turn up in the English Fens as eel grigs. Flat willow baskets on a hazel frame designed to drain and serve potatoes are traditional in Monmouthshire. Until recently, the French were still making basket 'bug traps' to slip under your pillow. Most countries have a form of the knapsack basket – you'll find it as a *hotte* in France, *kiepen* in Germany and *gerlo* in Italy. If you are a beginner and thinking of making one of these more unusual basket styles, round baskets are the simplest to make and cultivated willow the easiest and least frustrating material to use.

Hedgerow baskets are becoming popular, using stripped stems of hazel, dogwood, holly and other wild material found to be long and pliable enough. This is collected late in the year and usually stored in a damp place until spring, but sometimes it is used straight from the bush or tree complete with buds and cones for added interest. The results of all these subtle shades and textures are beautiful but rather unpredictable – wild material can be a bit wayward so don't expect the finished item to be completely symmetrical or easy to work.

Today the keen amateur might try making a large sturdy basket – a linen basket or picnic hamper, trays and baskets with wooden bases, holders, stands or small racks.

Rushwork has an equally long history dating back at least 8000 years according to archaeological evidence in Palestine and Jordan. It is not surprising that rushes with their strong but pliable green stems have been valued throughout history for such a wide variety of uses, from a sturdy woven chair for an Egyptian Pharaoh, to the more recent cheap rushlights, dipped in rancid butter or hog's fat for those who could not afford the luxury of wax candles. A length of about 60 cm/2 feet would burn for about an hour.

Rushes are easily obtainable and do not need cultivating to maintain a good supply, since the large freshwater rush, *Scirpus lacustris*, which is the best species for plaiting and weaving, grows prolifically in rivers and in the shallows of lakes and ponds. The rushes are normally

SECTION ONE

harvested in summer every two years when they are about 2 metres/6 feet high above water level. They are cut from below water level using a curved reaping hook, either from a flat-bottomed boat or by wading into the water at waist level, taking care the stems don't get bent or they will break later when dried.

Rushes are usually rinsed clear of mud and dirt, then left to dry on the ground or stacked in loose bundles. They must be dried carefully – direct sunlight will bleach the rushes and make them brittle, while drying too quickly may cause them to shrink later and make the work loose. Rain and damp can cause mould.

Before carpets became customary, rich and poor alike used rushes to cover the rather damp and dirty earth or stone floors of hall and hovel; the hardy sweet flag, *Acorus calamus variegatus*, with its fresh, sweet smell when crushed was preferred for this purpose, often mixed with scented 'strewing' herbs such as *Santolina*, meadowsweet and lavender. The rushes could be swept away and replaced with fresh ones periodically, removing all the collected dirt and debris. Changing the rushes even took on a ritual significance with the traditional rush-bearing ceremonies still held annually in some English villages.

Later, during the Middle Ages, rushes were also used extensively as a floor covering, but by then, were being plaited and woven into mats by coiling a long plait and sewing it together until the required size was reached: a simple but effective technique that is still popular for making rush mats today. From here, it wasn't long before plaiting and weaving methods were developed to extend rushwork into bedding and seating, more adventurous and decorative matting, bags, baskets, hats, and even horse collars. Rushes were found useful for strengthening the plasterwork in the walls of buildings and in many regions where rushes were plentiful, are still the traditional material for thatching a roof.

Modern cane and rush seating workshop – it has remained unchanged in appearance and operation for over a century

STYLE GUIDE

SECTION ONE

Making rush-seated chairs became popular in the early eighteenth century and had developed into a flourishing cottage industry by the late nineteenth century, particularly in some parts of Britain where one small village might have been turning them out in their thousands. These chairs were often used in halls and churches; this is probably why so many can still be found and why, after such communal use, most are in great need of repair.

Men generally made the wooden frames, usually from ash, while the women made the rush seats in their homes, sitting on low stools or on the floor. They were called rush 'matters' and the job was considered unpleasant, the dried rushes being dusty and smelly and in need of soaking to make them pliable enough to use. The basic plaiting technique required little skill but assessing how many rushes were needed and exactly when to introduce a new rush to maintain an even thickness, demanded attention, experience and good judgement. There were also itinerant 'rush bottomers' who travelled from town to village, re-seating any worn or damaged rushwork, often at the side of the road.

The soft, pliable nature of rushes makes them ideal for chair seats; the seat should be padded, raised slightly above the edges of the chair frame and traditionally stuffed with broken rushes pushed between the woven seat covering for extra comfort. This also adds strength and tightens up the weaving. During their heyday in the nineteenth century a great many styles of rush-seated chairs were produced from folding and cane-backed types, to rocking chairs, babies' high chairs, dining and easy chairs. Old catalogues show that one company alone might offer hundreds of different variations of style.

The novice rush worker might start with a simple check-weave tablemat and progress to baskets, holders, perhaps even a rush hat (moulded round a hat block which could be improvised from stiff paper) to get used to handling the material before tackling a chair seat. Although the basic seating technique is the same, seats vary in shape and can be square, rectangular or trapezium-shaped, narrowing towards the back.

STYLE GUIDE

The type of cane used as a seating material came originally from China where bamboo chairs with cane seats were common, and became popular in the Western world in the seventeenth century. Rattan cane from Malay was soon being imported in large quantities for chair seating, particularly in France and Holland where the style became very elegant and refined despite the fact that the technique had remained unchanged 'for thousands of years – rush-seated stools and a beautiful caned day-bed are among the Tutankhamun treasures.

Cane furniture has enjoyed periods of great popularity ever since its seventeenth-century heyday and especially in the late nineteenth century when there was a great surge of interest in oriental furniture resulting in as many as 150 specialist manufacturers in Britain alone. Most of the second-hand bamboo and cane period pieces available today date from between the mid-nineteenth century and 1930. The cane first used for chair backs and seats was the outside or glossy rattan cane, sometimes called chair-seating cane. In Europe the pulp centre was treated as waste although it would sometimes be made into cricket bat handles and whips. Later, the thin, round (pulp) cane became popular for turning into furniture to be painted or varnished.

Traditionally, cane has not only been used to make furniture: the waste fibre might be converted into mats, cheap upholstery stuffing or, in China, a covering for ginger jars. Cane's strong but pliable nature has lent itself to all kinds of receptacles from hampers and baskets to skeps for carrying coal, wood and cotton. You also find it in old cricket bat and tennis racket handles, hat brims and beer barrel spigots. In the tropical areas where cane grows, it might not only be used for sleeping mats, elephant gear and fishing traps, but also as a major building material for constructing huts, stockades and suspension bridges.

If you are re-seating a chair, the chances are that it will be an old one – a frame you have picked up at an auction or a damaged chair either inherited or found at the back of the attic. There are no hard-and-fast rules of thumb about cane and rushwork styles, although

SECTION ONE

some do incorporate idiosyncratic variations in design; some chairs had a beaded edging for example, others utilize pegs all round – there are no real historical or geographical patterns. Sometimes a shred of seating remains giving a clue to the pattern and type; otherwise, it is really up to you and you cannot go far wrong. Before removing any old canework, it is a good idea to make a note of the sizes of cane used and the type and size of beading, if any.

The most frequently used technique for seats is the 'double setting' pattern which is both strong and long-lasting (page 37). You sometimes see 'single setting' but it is not as strong or as rigid as the double design. You might find it useful to look at surviving chairs in museums such as the Chair Museum in High Wycombe (one of the old chair-making centres in the last century) which has a marvellous selection of country style originals; or to browse round antique shops studying different chairs.

Unlike chairs which lend themselves to repair, you are more likely to be making a basket from new, perhaps to meet a specific purpose or because you have found a new use for that particular size and shape. However, there is a need for basket repairs, perhaps for a much loved or much used basket; even an antique hamper or fruit basket. Old baskets have a wonderful deep colour and patina that is difficult to match if you are trying to repair a section or to fix new handles. In such cases you should choose your materials carefully to match in size and colour as closely as possible. I have sometimes resorted to cheating by using different coloured wood stains applied with a soft cloth to age the new section prematurely. You will find full instructions for basket repairs on page 76.

TOOLS AND

TECHNIQUES

◆ TOOLS AND MATERIALS ◆

The tools required for cane and willow work, particularly of a specialist nature, are fairly minimal and most can be improvised. After all, these crafts were originally carried out by people who would not have had the money to buy expensive equipment even if it had been available.

Tools for caning. From left to right: four different-sized bradawls and doublers, picking knife and mallet.

19

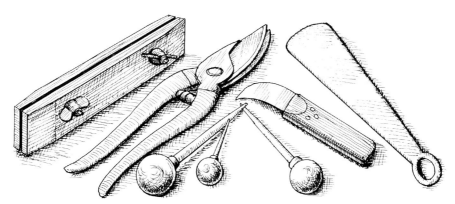

Tools for basketwork. From left to right: screwblock, heavy duty shears, three bodkins, knife and beating iron.

One of the most important things to remember when working with rush and willow particularly, is that they are never worked dry; cane may sometimes need to be dampened with a spray or wet towel if you are worried about getting enough tension for doubling, but should be dry for setting as it loses its natural slipperiness when wet and doesn't cross easily. Willow (and hedgerow material) must be well soaked before it becomes sufficiently pliable to work easily.

You should also bear in mind that unfinished baskets will have to be stored in a bath of water or a damp environment to avoid their distorting or drying out and cracking before the job is finished. An old tin bath or trough is ideal for willow depending on the lengths you will be working with – a hand spray is also useful to dampen any that may dry out while work is in progress.

Consider too your working environment. Many basket-makers prefer to work outdoors if the weather is damp. They generally work seated on the floor or ground, sometimes with a light board resting in a sloping position on their knees to which the basket can be fastened during construction. Others prefer to use a sloping board on a table; two pieces of wood 30 × 20 cm/12 × 8 inches and 20 × 15 cm/8 × 6 inches nailed together are ideal.

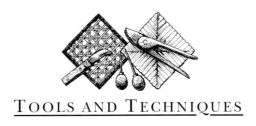

TOOLS AND TECHNIQUES

TOOLS FOR CANE AND WILLOW WORK

Bent bodkin: a large bodkin is useful for making a space to insert the handle on baskets. Other sizes are handy for threading material, opening spaces in the weave and so on.

Bradawl: used for pegging a cane base to a board so that it can be turned freely.

Caning knife: every chair caner has their personal caning knife, used mainly to help to thread the cane through. Few traditional caners had the funds to buy a special knife, so, as today, it would be an ordinary kitchen knife without its wooden handle and with the blade filed down.

Doublers: a range of different sized doublers are useful for making different sized holes when re-seating. Again, these are usually improvised by finding an old piece of wood turning and inserting a nail or knitting needle.

Mallet: used in chair work for clearing the frame of old cane or rushwork and for pegging.

Picking knife: useful for cutting off ends when the item is finished.

Rapping iron: tool like a thick metal file used for tapping the weaving rows of a basket into a level, evenly spaced position and for keeping the work close woven.

Round-nosed pliers: used for crushing or bruising basket stakes to make them easier to bend for bordering at a sharp angle without cracking.

Screwblock: stout wooden base which holds stakes in position when doing square-work.

SECTION TWO

Sharp knife: basket-makers' knives are available in various sizes for trimming ends, pointing stakes and other useful tasks.

Small bodkin: used to make the spaces in which to insert the stakes when basket-making.

TOOLS FOR RUSHWORK

Awl: flattened stick suitable for tucking in the ends and packing the work into shape; some use a similarly shaped piece of metal.

Tools for rushwork: needle (above) and stuffing stick (below).

Sharp knife: for cutting out an old seat – old worn rush can be surprisingly tough. You might also need an old screwdriver and a heavy hammer for removing rush from behind the bars of some old chair frames.

Stuffing stick: a piece of surplus timber for pushing loose rushes into the base of the seat to pad it.

TOOLS AND TECHNIQUES

TYPES OF MATERIAL

Enamelled cane: a glossy flat cane available in lengths of 2 metres/6 feet in a choice of bright enamelled colours.

Pulp cane: the centre core of the rattan is circular and is the main type used for making baskets and for pegging cane-seated chairs. Sometimes called *segah,* it is available in various sizes identified by a number and can be dyed different colours, then used with natural cane to create attractive patterns and traditional effects. It is not really

Rattan cane is the best for reseating work.

SECTION TWO

pulpy, but strong and fibrous, yet still pliable.

To harvest, selected canes are washed, then passed through mechanized rollers which press the cane against knives to split and strip the outer sheath into narrow strips. These are planed on the back and sides to use for weaving items such as bedroom chair seats. The stripped cane passes to another machine which splits it into various sizes from $1\,\text{mm}/\frac{1}{16}$ inch to $18\,\text{mm}/1\frac{1}{4}$ inches in diameter. Other machines can split or cut the cane into a variety of shapes: square, flat, bevelled or half-round.

Cane is largely processed in Germany and North America, although France, Holland and Italy also have thriving cane-splitting industries. The canes can be split by hand as they are in China but the results are rough and poor quality. Incidentally, the knotted roots of the cane are not suitable for splitting and are usually made into polo balls and mallets.

Rattan cane: a climbing or trailing plant, also known as cane palm, native to tropical jungles and swamps which grows 60–185 metres/ 200–600 feet long with a diameter of 2.5 cm/1 inch or less. The best is found in Malaysia and Indonesia and while it is sometimes cultivated in the former country, it is usually gathered from the wild. Rattan is also found in West Africa and other tropical countries.

Leaves appear only on the ends of the shoots. Young plants hold themselves erect until they are several feet long, then they need supporting; they use feelers or hooked thorns called flagellum to cling to other plants. The outer sheath or bark is also thorny so thick hide gloves are worn for harvesting. This is done by severing the branches with a small axe.

The branches are left to hang until the sun has shrivelled and loosened the outer bark. The cane can then be removed by cutting a notch in the trunk of a neighbouring tree and drawing the cane through it, thus removing the bark. The inner bark is hard and glossy.

The cane is usually cut into lengths from 3.5 metres/12 feet to 9

TOOLS AND TECHNIQUES

metres/30 feet and tied in bundles to be shipped to Singapore for grading, then sold through agents to China, America, Germany, Holland, France and England. It is sold in a variety of widths coded by numbers: No. 1 is the finest; Nos. 2 and 3 are the most commonly used sizes; then there is No. 4 for a heavier effect and No. 6 which is usually used for beading. Rattan is generally supplied in bundles weighing 250 g/9 oz. The cane should be stored flat on a rack or looped and hung away from any source of heat which may cause it to turn brittle and crack.

Rattan is sometimes called glossy or chair-seating cane: it is glossy on one side and is worked so that this lies uppermost on the seat.

Rush: lengths vary from 1.2 metres/4 feet to 1.8 metres/6 feet, tapering at one end. Rush can be plaited for strength, giving its pleasant sage green colour an attractive textured appearance. The bulrush, *Scirpus lacustris*, grows in rivers, streams and ponds and is harvested in clumps or stands every other year to allow for regrowth. If you are cutting your own (as close to the roots as possible), they need to dry in the open air or under a shelter for about one to three weeks depending on the weather (page 35). Alternatively, you can buy rush in bundles or 'bolts' weighing about 2 kg/ $4\frac{1}{2}$ lb. Each bolt contains a variety of sizes.

Rushes can also be imported from Holland: the freshwater species are long and soft while the salt-water type are harder, browner and shorter. If you wish to experiment, any plant with long, strap-like leaves might be used: yellow flag iris, the English reedmace (or false bulrush) and gladiolus are all worthy candidates.

Straw plait: an inexpensive material used for weaving cheap baskets over cane stakes.

Twisted seagrass: naturally a bronze green colour, this is also available in brighter, dyed shades for weaving over cane stakes.

SECTION TWO

Willow: also called osier, grows best in well-drained, rich soil close to water. It enjoys occasional flooding but does not flourish in stagnant water. For basket-making, the osiers are grown in regularly spaced rows of spiky stumps or 'stools' which throw out a spray of quick-growing shoots in early spring.

The resulting slender stems are cut by hand with a sickle or reaping hook before winter. The cut stems are called rods and although some are used as they are, after grading to length, tying loosely in bundles and leaving to dry in a dry, open well-ventilated place, most are processed for the basket and hurdle trade. Brown willow, as the untreated rods are called, is mostly used for work that will be exposed to damp such as garden furniture, fish and vegetable baskets, and in some instances, creative wickerwork garden statuary. 'Green' rods are similar – these are cut in the summer and used unseasoned for crab and lobster pots, and salmon and eel traps.

However, most willow is used 'white' – that is with the bark stripped off. This is usually done in spring as the sap is rising and before the leaves open, meaning the osiers have to be cut late. Stripping the willow was traditionally a job carried out by women and children who used a special tool called a stripping brake for the job. Nowadays there are machines which will strip several rods at a time. The newly peeled rods are dried in the open, stood against posts or laid along the hedgerows. You will also find a type of willow called 'buffs'. These are boiled in water and allowed to soak for several hours before stripping, resulting in a reddish brown colour taken from the tannin in the bark.

Willow is sold by the length, not the thickness as with cane. Lengths run by the metre or foot from 1 metre/3 feet upwards, tied in bundles or bolts about 1 metre/3 feet round at the base. Some suppliers sell smaller amounts but usually only to clubs or classes. Willow must be stored dry and only soaked prior to use to restore pliability.

Wooden bases: sometimes used for making baskets and basketwork trays, they are traditionally made of oak or birch (less expensive but with less

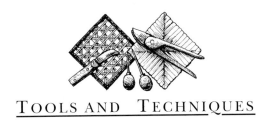

Tools and Techniques

timber-grain interest), you can also buy plastic or non-warp plywood bases. Bases are sometimes given a coloured or special finish (page 28).

CANE NAMES

There are about 300 known types of cane. The following is a selection of the main trade names.

Boon doot: a hard, slightly ribbed cane with a light red/brown colour.

Kooboo: (the Malay word for trap or stockade since these are generally made of cane) a yellow glossy cane popular for hampers.

Malacca: best known for walking sticks, this cane is not quite round having a slight rib on one side. The leaf joints can be as much as 1.5 metres/5 feet apart. Stiffer than rattan, malacca is also used for drain rods and chimney sweep's canes.

Nilghiri: a very hard, difficult to bend cane which grows in India. Used mainly for walking sticks.

Palembang: a red/brown cane with a slightly ribbed surface. The coarser variety may be used for hampers and baskets; the finer is popular (after washing) for chairs.

Sarawak: a good quality, glossy surfaced cane: the outer part is used for seating and the inner pulp for bat handles.

Segah: a fine glossy cane used for chair seating and as pulp cane.

Tohiti: a stout cane used for furniture frames and stiffening hampers.

◆ PREPARATION TECHNIQUES ◆

As with any craft, good preparation is essential for a successful finish. With most basket-making and chair seating however, providing the necessary materials are to hand and your work space is well organized, very little preparation work is necessary. The exceptions are when you might be incorporating a wooden basket base which may need staining and varnishing or painting; or when you are re-seating an old chair and know the frame requires attention. It is always a good idea to select all the relevant elements required before you start, picking out and checking the best materials and putting them close at hand.

FINISHES FOR WOODEN BASES

Bases are usually stained and polished although they are sometimes painted or enamelled. The surface must be perfectly smooth before you start, so rub it over with fine sandpaper and wipe with a damp cloth. Your chosen stain should be applied as evenly as possible with a soft brush or cloth and worked in the same direction as the grain of the timber. Allow to dry completely, then rub down again lightly with the finest grade sandpaper. Repeat this procedure until the necessary depth of colour is achieved, then after the final sanding, apply the polish or varnish.

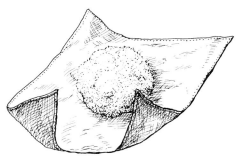

Make a wad by wrapping a small bundle of absorbent cotton in a piece of lint-free material – such as a large handkerchief.

French polish requires a warm, dry atmosphere, preferably in a temperature of about 21°C/70°F. The varnish is brushed on to the wood and allowed to soak in and dry for about an hour. After lightly sanding and wiping free from any dust with a damp cloth, the polish is then applied using a wad of scalded and dried muslin or lint-free cotton, soaked in but not saturated with, polish. A little linseed oil is dabbed on the bottom of the pad to keep it moving freely and then this is worked into the base using a series of small circular motions until the surface of the base is covered.

As the pad dries out, more polish and a trace more linseed oil is applied to aid a good gliding action. After several applications, the base should be left to dry for several hours. The final process is to buff up the polish, sometimes called 'spiriting off'. This is designed to remove any smears. Using methylated spirit on your pad, you wipe lightly in the direction of the grain of the wood, just enough to remove any marks without wiping away the polish.

Alternatively, you could apply several coats of polyurethane varnish instead of French polishing – matt, silk or shiny finish are preferred. Tinted varnishes are now available if you wish to change the hue subtly or omit the staining stage. To apply varnish successfully, always make sure you have wiped away any excess from the brush and apply lightly

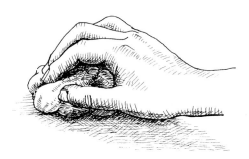

Finish off with a clean pad dipped in methylated spirits and worked lightly with the grain.

and evenly in the direction of the grain. Allow to dry thoroughly before applying the next coat. Several thin coats are always better than one thick one which is more likely to show up streaks and unevenness.

Sometimes basket (and tray) bases are enamelled; in this case, those made in birch are usually preferred as they have a much closer grain for a smooth finish. The surface is sanded and wiped as before, then a coat of quick-drying enamel is applied. Up to three thin coats will be necessary to create the depth of colour: never apply the enamel thickly or you will get ugly runs and brushmarks.

PREPARING A CHAIR FOR RE-SEATING

If you have acquired an old frame for re-seating, do check that it does not require any essential repairs before you start work. If the chair legs are of uneven length for example, do not be tempted to even them up by sawing off sections from the longer ones: you might end up with a chair which not only looks out of proportion, but is also too low for sitting at a table. It is preferable to build up the short leg by gluing or screwing on a slip of hardwood.

Repairing a broken leg.

Glue break together.

Or smooth off the jagged edges and insert a dowel.

TOOLS AND TECHNIQUES

*Make sure that all your material is conveniently at
hand before you start work.*

SECTION TWO

A broken leg can often be repaired by gluing the two parts back together again. If this does not seem strong enough, the repair might be reinforced with a wooden dowel. When the glue is dry, you could saw the leg in two just above or below the glued fracture, and drill out the centre of both sections so a long dowel can be inserted for additional strength. Worm or damp damage is probably best left to an expert for treatment and repair.

More usually though, it is the joints that have simply loosened where the glue holding the frame together has perished. The best solution in such a case is to knock the joints gently apart using a mallet protected with a rag or piece of thick card. It is a good idea to label the sections first for easy reassembly. Gently file off any existing glue until the joints fit together smoothly, then reglue using cramps (such as lengths of string) to hold the chair in position until the glue has dried.

Always take extra care knocking the joints apart if the chair is a very old one and likely to be fragile. Where only a couple of joints are loose, it is sometimes possible to glue them without knocking the whole frame apart.

A chair will often seem rickety if one of the rails which serve to strengthen and reinforce the chair legs has become dislodged or broken. If the rail has simply been knocked out of its hole, a hardwood dowel fixed through the leg and the rail end should secure it back in place. Where the rail has broken through, it may possibly be reglued if the break is a clean one; but mostly, for sufficient strength, you will have to replace it with a new, matching rail or ask a carpenter to make a new one to match. You will need to remove the old rail with a tenon saw, drill out the remaining stubs and clean the holes with a small file.

The new rail must be cut to length, remembering to allow for the ends which enter the legs. So that they fit snugly, the diameter of the holes in the legs should be measured and a circle of the same diameter drawn on the new rail using compasses. File the ends of the rail until they are the right size to fit the holes tightly. Apply

32

TOOLS AND TECHNIQUES

woodworking adhesive to both the holes and ends of the rail, gently pull the chair legs apart and fit the rail into position. Try not to let the other rails slip out while the legs are eased apart. When any excess glue has been wiped away, a length of fabric or piece of string wound around the chair legs will hold the rail in place until the glue has set. If you are worried about this marking the wood on the legs, insert cotton wool pads where the pressure of the string or tourniquet will be the greatest. When the adhesive has set and the ties have been removed, the rail can be stained or varnished to match the finish of the rest of the chair.

Cane-seated chairs sometimes develop a split along the line of caning holes. If this has happened, run a line of glue into the split and use screws driven from inside the frame between the holes to support the rail.

Where one of the seat rails of a rush-seated chair has cracked, it is a relatively simple job to replace it by making a new one using chisels and a surform plane. Try to copy the original shape as closely as possible. The rail may also need staining and distressing – prematurely ageing by sanding and scratching or bashing with hard objects – to match the rest of the chair.

Sometimes an item may have been painted or varnished – especially simple country chairs – and you would like to strip it. There are various proprietary solutions on the market; always follow the manufacturer's instruction carefully and wear protective clothing. Stripping usually involves painting on some chemical thickly and waiting for the paint to pucker and bubble. It can then be removed using a chisel scraper or special scraping tool; sharpened pieces of scrap wood are sometimes useful for awkward crevices. Several applications of stripper may be necessary.

When most of the paint has been removed, a ball of coarse steel wool usually finishes the job off; take care only to use this in the direction of the grain of the wood to avoid scratch marks. Any residue should be cleaned away with white spirit and the piece allowed to dry.

SECTION TWO

Country furniture was sometimes painted with milk paint – a popular treatment in the eighteenth century. Made of boiled-down buttermilk and animal blood, it is usually impervious to modern strippers and you will have to use a strong ammonia solution applied with wire wool and left to soak in. This should loosen the paint which can then be scraped away.

REPAIRING OR REMOVING OLD CANEWORK

Where canework remains undamaged – maybe in a chair back or in some of a set of chairs that need repairing, you will find that it tends to darken with age and go a deeper shade of brown. You can reproduce this effect when re-caning antique furniture by brushing on a strong concentration of analine walnut stain in methylated spirit, then wiping off with an old rag, leaving a darker concentration in the corners.

Old canework naturally attracts a lot of dirt and dust in all those crevices; warm soapy water and a stiff bristled brush are usually the most effective way to clean it up. Alternatively, if the dirt is really ingrained, you might try wetting the whole area with warm water and applying white baking powder with an old paintbrush. When this has dried, brush off, wash with cold water and allow to dry naturally.

Occasionally, antique canework may have been protected with a coat of varnish which tends to darken and flake off in patches. If steel wool doesn't remove it totally, resort gingerly to paint stripper, taking care that you don't get any on the wooden frame and protecting your hands with rubber gloves. Any remaining areas of varnish can usually be removed with a little white spirit on a soft rag.

The odd broken strand can be repaired by sticking a new length as a patch between the break at the back using a quick-drying acrylic adhesive. If the damage is extensive, the whole section of canework will have to be cut away and replaced – don't forget to take careful note of the colour and pattern of the original weave.

TOOLS AND TECHNIQUES

If the canework is very damaged and you have to remove it totally, it is a good idea to make a note of the size and pattern, and keep a small piece for colour matching – the new panel when completed can be stained to a matching shade. Cut around the panel close to the inside of the frame with a sharp knife, taking care not to damage the wood. Using a clearing tool suited to the thickness of the hole – about three quarters of its size is ideal – and a light hammer, remove any old canework and pegs from the holes around the frame.

You should work from underneath the frame taking especial care at the corners in case the holes run at an angle. In some chairs the corner holes may also be blind and not go right the way through. You may be able to pull out the old cane from the top or remove it carefully with a hand drill. Once all the holes are clear, clean the frame with a little turpentine and check it for damage. Any possible repairs should be made at this stage; check particularly for any badly damaged caning holes as it would be pointless to continue if the frame were irreparable.

PREPARATION FOR WORKING WITH WILLOW

Having selected the material you need for each stage of a particular job, soak the willow rods in cold or warm (not hot) water depending on the type and size. Whites and buffs need shorter soaking time than browns; warmer water speeds up the process – whites will only need a brief dip if you are using warm water. After soaking, the rods are stood on their butt (thicker) ends, to drain, then laid, covered with a damp blanket or sacking, in a draught-free but unheated place.

PREPARATION FOR WORKING WITH CANE

After selecting your lengths of cane, examine them carefully for any flaws. You should look for discoloured patches, weak or brittle joints or weak areas. Cane can be worked damp for doubling but this should not be necessary if you are using good quality cane.

SECTION TWO

PREPARATION FOR WORKING WITH RUSH

It is best to sort out what size rushes you think you will need before starting – too thin or small could look inadequate and not be sufficiently strong. When you have made your selection, the rushes must be pre-dampened before use. If they are good quality, a thorough sprinkling from a hosepipe or watering can, then wrapping in a damp sheet or blanket until pliable is usually sufficient. This may take from one to three hours depending on the type and conditions – English reedmace and water iris are very quick to soften, while Continental types usually take longer. The rushes are ready when they can be bent or twisted in any direction without cracking or breaking.

If the weather is particularly hot and dry or the rushes are rather hard and brittle, it may be advisable to soak them first in a trough of water although this should be a last resort as they do not usually respond well to being totally submersed for any length of time. Again it may take anything between one and four hours to make them pliable; lay in a cool place to drain for about 30 minutes.

Only dampen what you estimate you will need for the moment as you can only repeat the damping and drying process a few times before the rushes start to become discoloured and soggy. Damp rushes should remain usable in a bundle for several days without re-soaking. Some rushworkers recommend wiping each rush before use and snapping off the tips in case they are too thin and brittle for weaving but this only really applies to the dirtiest and smallest of rushes.

$\mathcal{P}$ROJECTS

◆ DOUBLE-CANED CHAIR SEAT ◆

The doubled-setting design is far stronger and more durable than single caning and is certainly the most common both to be found on old chairs or chosen for new ones. It involves interweaving pairs of canes from front to back and from side to side of the frame, with a further pattern of single cane woven diagonally across each square. This technique can be adapted to any size or shape of chair or stool from squares and rectangles to awkwardly shaped corner seats. There are a couple of more decorative or stronger designs developed for a certain purpose, as described in Projects Two and Three (pages 46 and 51).

Before you start, do check that the chair frame is sound and make sure there are no remaining shreds of old caning (page 34). Then assemble the correct size and amount of cane you need and lay or hang it where it will be conveniently at hand. The cane is usually supplied in hanks weighing 250 g/9 oz; or you can sometimes purchase all you need to complete one average chair seat from your local craft shop. Buy Nos. 2 and 3 flat seating cane for the main work, No. 6 for the beading. Any short lengths – perhaps where a cane has split or broken – can be reserved for couching, the term for binding the beading that neatens the underside of the chair.

1 The first process when recaning a chair is called doubling and you will be working from top to bottom of your frame. First find the centre holes at the top and bottom of the frame and insert a length of string

to make sure it is truly vertical. From that centre point, start threading your piece of cane in and out from top to bottom, working towards the right-hand side of the frame.

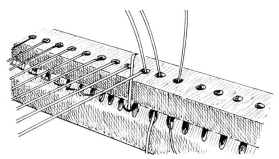

Threading the cane through the holes of the frame.

Every time you thread the cane through, pull it tight, and insert a 'doubler' – a screwdriver type of tool – into the hole to prevent it from slipping while you thread the cane through the next hole. Tighten and insert a doubler in this hole, then continue in this fashion until you finish the whole right-hand side of the frame. If the frame is not square, you will have to complete a few shorter lengths down the side.

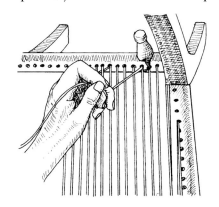

Doubling runs from top to bottom of the frame.

Doubling completed – note the short lengths to accommodate the sides.

PROJECTS

As good as new – antique country chair with new rush seat.

2 When you get to the last hole on the right, loop the cane underneath and thread it back through; then start working back towards the centre in exactly the same manner, using doublers to hold the cane tight and working up and down. On reaching the left-hand side of the frame, loop and thread as before, then work back to the centre where you first started. Tuck the end of the cane under one of the other doublings on the underside of the seat and cut it off.

3 The next stage is called setting and it involves working the cane from left to right. It is very important that you have the same number of holes on both sides of the chair – there is no point in proceeding if the frame is faulty. Start at the back with a piece of cane, poking it into the hole of the nearest doubler to hold it. Start working across the frame from left to right, inserting the cane over one doubling and underneath the next, all the way along. See page 42.

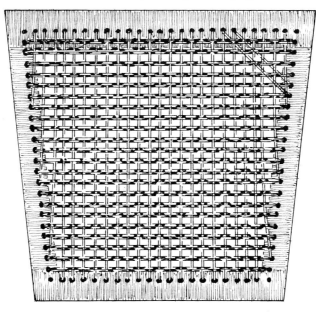

Doubling and setting completed.

4 When you get to the far side, leave that end of cane loose and insert a fresh piece as before; then start working across the frame, feeding the cane over and under until you reach the left-hand side. It is important always to start by threading the cane over to get the right pattern effect. When you get to the other side, thread the cane through the last hole and up the next and put in a doubler. Start working back again left to right with the same piece. Continue backwards and forwards using the two pieces of cane at the same time.

Settings work the cane horizontally across the doublings.

5 When all the horizontals are completed, you can 'straighten up' – this simply means taking a look at the work at arms' length and adjusting by hand to ensure the pattern lies square.

Working on the settings – the horizontal lines of canes.

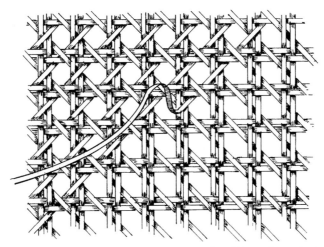

Crossing produces the distinctive double-setting design.

6 To complete the web effect, the final stage is called 'crossing' when the cane is worked in a diagonal direction. Starting at any corner with a fresh piece of cane, you thread it over the verticals and under the horizontals all the way across until you reach the other side. Tuck the end down into a hole (no need to loop it) and cut it off.

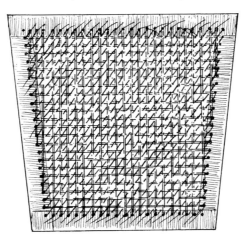

Crossings completed in one direction.

7 Then work your crossings in the opposite direction, passing under the verticals and over the horizontals this time. In each hole there will be two crossings – the one that passed over the vertical the first time, tied in by the second. When you have finished all the diagonal crossings in both directions, go right round and make sure all the ends are tucked in.

Crossings are worked across the diagonal.

8 To finish off, you split some soft wood such as deal (like kindling wood) down to the size of your frame holes using a hammer and Stanley knife. Make the pieces into neat round pegs or dowels and put a peg in each alternate hole around the frame, but leaving the corner one free. Thus you always start with the third hole along.

PROJECTS

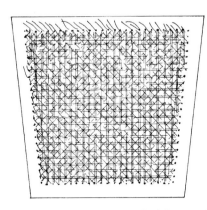

After crossing, go round and tidy up the ends.

9 When you have pegged all the way round, you take a piece of No. 6 cane cut to the length you need, and some slender No. 2 cane as your couching. The couching loops through the holes, to hold the beading in place. Finish with a peg in each corner hole to hold the beading firm. You may have seen some old chairs which do not have beading and where all the holes are pegged instead – take your cue from how the seat was finished previously, or finish whichever way you prefer as there are no rigid historical rules as to which is correct.

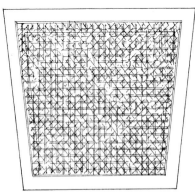

Tied and pegged beading finishes off the underside of a cane-seated chair.

Joining Cane

When you need to join two pieces of cane, take the original piece that you are working with and insert it up the next hole; feed the new piece of cane down the same hole, then loop the new piece underneath the old and fold it back on itself. This results in two pieces coming up out of the same hole. Tuck the old piece under an adjacent doubling and carry on with the new. You can be confident the two ends will hold tight.

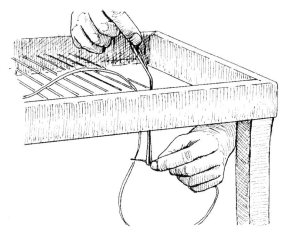

Joining a new piece of cane.

Project Two

◆ SPIDER-BACKED CHAIR ◆

The effect of the spider-backed chair is attractive and rather unusual yet seen fairly frequently in old, more ornamental chairs. It features a central wooden medallion, often intricately decorated. This is held in place by a 'spider's web' of cane and should have the same number of holes as the external chair frame so that it can be directly fastened to it. The holes in the medallion tend to be very fine and rather close together so check carefully for any damage before you start.

PROJECTS

*The spider-backed chair incorporates a decorative
wooden medallion.*

SECTION THREE

Probably part of the old caning will be in existence, holding the disc in place and this will have to be carefully removed as described on page 34, making sure that the holes are cleared of any pegs and old bits of cane without damaging them. Often the medallion is lacquered so be especially careful when cleaning off any dirt and grease – use only a damp cloth, never any proprietary cleaning agent. If this is not sufficiently effective, consult a professional furniture restorer if necessary, to avoid damaging the lacquer.

1 Before you can start caning, the medallion will have to be temporarily supported in its rightful place. You could make a special wooden brace and screw it into position. Alternatively, take four lengths of stiffish wire cut to the correct length and thread these through the top, bottom and centre side holes. The other end of each wire is then fixed to the corresponding centre hole in each side of the frame. When this is done, double check with a tape measure that the medallion is positioned exactly in the centre, and that any design or picture is not upside down.

2 The technique is more or less the same as for conventional caning (see Project One, page 37), except that the cane is worked in a circular direction. For stability it is a good idea to put a little spot of glue between the canes every time they cross.

The first double settings are threaded to radiate out from the central medallion, starting one hole to the left of the central top supporting wire in the frame. Proceed as for doubling, putting one cane of each pair in first: pass the cane down to the first hole to the left of the top supporting wire in the medallion; pass it through the next hole to the left in the medallion, then up to the next hole to the left in the frame.

In this way, the work can continue in an anticlockwise direction until you reach the point where you started and the frame is filled with cane spokes. Tighten the canes as much as you can without pulling the

medallion out of place. You can remove the supporting wires as you go round completing the caning.

3 Using the same cane, then reverse the direction, adding the second cane of each pair as you work clockwise around the frame. You will finish at the centre hole in the top of the frame: tie in the loose ends at the back of the frame.

4 The settings are worked around the frame in a circular motion. Start in the lower left-hand side of the medallion with a pair of setting canes and weave them over and under your 'spoke' doubles until the frame is filled; remember that as with the basic technique described for setting on page 40, the first cane of each pair (that is, the one nearest the medallion) passes over-under, over-under, while the second moves in reverse: under-over. The corners can be worked with short lengths of cane where necessary to fill any spaces. Take care to check your work frequently to ensure the cane remains taut and evenly spaced. Any discrepancy will show up as a distortion of the design when the caning is completed.

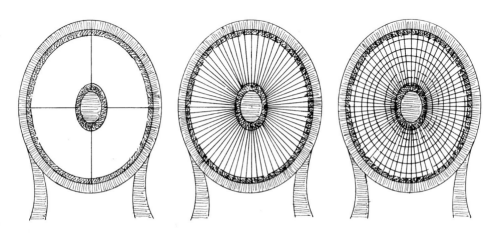

Medallion with first and second settings completed

5 Each crossing cane is worked from the central medallion out to the appropriate hole in the frame. The first cane should be worked under the first left-hand settings and over the second, curving backwards in an anticlockwise direction. When you reach the corners, try to space the canes as evenly as possible.

When the crossings are completed, the ends are tucked in as before, then the holes around the frame pegged using pulp or round centre cane (or cut pegs of beechwood) and the finest slivers of cane for pegging the smaller holes of the medallion.

Willowing

You may sometimes see canework chairs which display the most beautifully intricate patterns and designs, usually on the backs. This is called 'willowing' and involves a totally different technique. There are

A fine example of willow work – but beyond the beginner.

no holes for the cane to be threaded through and the horizontals are worked first by knotting and tying in. It is a very advanced procedure that only an experienced caneworker would feel confident enough to tackle; even a professional would take about 16 hours to complete the job, compared with $2\frac{1}{2}$ to finish a conventional double-set seat.

PROJECT THREE

◆ CLOSE-CANED SEAT ◆

Close-caning is a variation on the basic caning technique which produces a very dense pattern. It is particularly suitable for an absolutely square seat such as a stool. As well as being strong, it is less easy to see through – which was why this style was once popular for commode seats.

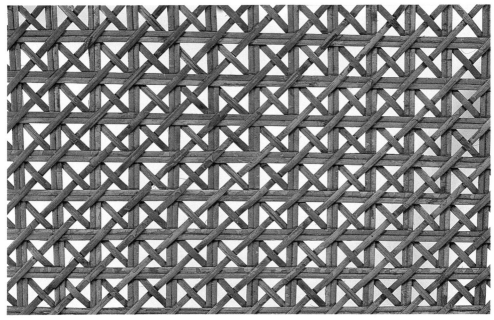

Close-caning – usually used for commode seats.

1 You insert your double settings along the verticals as usual, but when you come to the horizontal settings, you lay them on top of the first canes instead of weaving them in and out.

2 Then starting at the front of the chair frame – left or right corner, it doesn't matter which – insert your cane not in the corner hole, but the next one along in whichever direction you are going. Pass it up to the second hole of the vertical side of the frame, then back down to the bottom again and so on until you reach the top corner on the opposite side.

3 When you reach the end, put the cane down the adjacent hole and using short lengths for each diagonal, go over and under until all the settings are tied in and the frame is finished. Finish with pegs and/or beading as described on page 45.

PROJECT FOUR

◆ RUSH MATS ◆

Rush mats are relatively easy to make and will accustom you to working with the material. Make up a whole set or just some new mats to replace worn or damaged ones in an existing set. The colour of new mats soon mellows as the rushes dry out but much of their charm is in the variation you get in khaki, buff and sage shades.

This design uses the basic rush weaving techniques: mainly a pairing weave with a plain threadaway border and a check-weave centre. Each mat which measures 18 cm/7 inches in diameter, will require 10 medium sized rushes to use as stakes and 15 weavers, thinner than your stakes. The length of your stakes should be equal to the diameter of the mat plus 25 cm/10 inches for the border. The cut-off ends can be used as weavers if they are not too thick. A few spares are useful in case of breakages.

PROJECTS

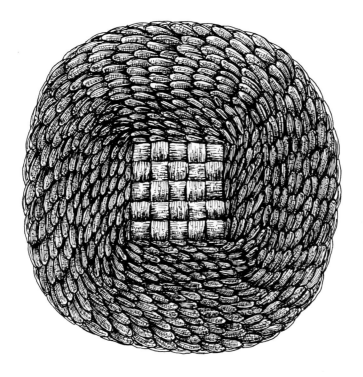

Finished mat with check-weave centre.

1 First make the basic framework of the mat by weaving the stakes over and under each other in a square: this is check-weaving. Lay five stakes close together in a row horizontally on your table or work surface, with the butts pointing in alternate directions to distribute the thickness more evenly.

2 Holding the stakes in position with one hand, pick up every alternate one and lay in the first vertical stake, to produce an over-and-under pattern. Lay down three horizontal stakes and holding the other two, lay down another vertical one, then weave in a third. Remember the butts and tips must be laid alternately.

SECTION THREE

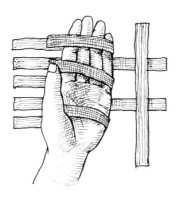

Starting the check-weave centre.

3 Change hands and weave in the remaining two stakes to the left of the centre, checking all the time that the weaving remains square. The weaving must be tight and level or it will become loose and gappy once the rushes dry and shrink.

4 The main part of the mat is linked to the check-weave centre with a plain close weave called pairing. First mark the top left-hand stake with a loop of coloured wool or string and working with two ends alternately, loop your weaver in half round this stake, bringing the ends towards you on top of the mat.

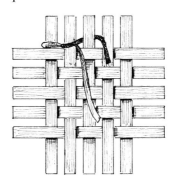

Pairing the rush.

5 Cross the left end over the right behind the second stake and out in the next space, pulling to tighten and bringing it forwards so that it lies parallel with the other one.

6 Then repeat the same action with the other half of the doubled weaver which lies to the left. Repeat with alternate ends until you reach the corner. Should the weaver break when you are tightening it – although it shouldn't if the rushes are well dampened and you pull firmly without snatching at them – simply cut a new one and thread it through your weaving tool, drawing it thus through the weave on top of the broken rush. Remove the broken weaver.

7 At the corner, give the mat a quarter turn to the left and work in the same manner along the second side, remembering to keep the weavers in the right order, working left over right and pulling tight as you progress. Work the next two sides in the same way, making sure you keep the same tension and that the stakes do not move out of position.

If you find the weaving is not lying very level or straight, use the threading tool to correct any bulges by pushing the rounded tip between each stake against the pairing while pulling the stakes firmly into position to maintain a neat square. The stakes should lie flat where they cross each other.

8 The main part of the mat is completed with a pairing technique producing a circular shape from your square centre. The two centre stakes forming a cross at the heart of your mat remain, but the others are splayed gently outwards to form the spokes of a wheel. These are secured in position as you continue to work round, the weaver pulled tight around them holding them in place.

9 Continue to work around the mat, turning it to the left and working along the top to keep the tension equal. When you need to

join a new weaver, stop when the shortest one is about 5 cm/2 inches long and keeping this to the right, loop the tip (never the butt – it will look too bulky) of your new weaver around the stake so that the long end lies alongside the short old one and the top against the new weaver. Pull the stake forward and slide the loop well down on the previous row so that it is hidden by the next stroke.

Joining in a new weaver.

10 Use the new tip and old weaver together for one looping – called a stroke – then make one stroke with the new weaver and short finished end. Continue weaving together until the ends are short enough to tuck under the mat to be trimmed off later. The join should be invisible. You can use the same technique should a weaver break by unpicking it to produce a length of about 5 cm/2 inches.

11 After a few rows, your mat will soon start taking on a circular shape – make sure the stakes are evenly spaced as you work by constantly pulling them into position. They should be completely hidden by the weavers. If the weaving is not pulled quite as tight as you

would like, use your threading tool to press it down tighter, pulling each stake outwards as you do so. Also take care to keep the weaving flat and do not allow it to curve into a bowl shape.

12 When the mat has reached the desired diameter (in this case 18 cm/7 inches), stop with the weavers on either side of the last stake. Push the threading tool into the weave about four rows down on top of the last stake and draw it out again at the edge of the work. Thread the right-hand weaver into the tool and pull down firmly on top of the last stake.

13 The remaining weaver makes a stroke over the last stake and behind the first to complete the round before threading it down in front of the first stake.

14 The border is a simple flat one and involves threading away the ends of the stakes like weavers. Each stake in turn is threaded behind the one on its right hand, then threaded away in front of it.

Threading away the border.

SECTION THREE

15 The last stake passes under the loop of the first and out to the front before going down in front of it, so leave the first loop a little slack to make this easier, then tighten up all round.

16 To finish, allow the mat to dry thoroughly before trimming away any ends with sharp pointed scissors. Give each stake a little tug before trimming off close to the weave; the end will spring back and disappear so don't pull too hard or it may unravel.

PROJECT FIVE

◆ RUSH SEAT ◆

The frame should be completely cleared of old rush. You may need to lever off any protective wooden slats on the sides, and if the nails are rusted in, prise them off with a hacksaw blade. Choose the rushes and soak them until pliable (page 35). You generally require about 1.5 kg/$3\frac{1}{4}$ lb of rush to complete a chair seat of about 38 cm/15 inches square. It helps to sit on a low stool or cushion when working so that you are at the right height to work on the chair comfortably. Lay your selected rushes conveniently to hand on the floor to your right.

1 Begin by picking up a rush and folding it over the back rail, then knotting it. Bring it towards the front and tie in two more rushes by their butts (thick ends) using a half-hitch knot. Twist these into a single strand by twisting them together in a clockwise direction – they should look like one finely twisted rush, not one wound round another. Press out the air as you go to prevent the rush looking bulky or uneven and pull as tight as you can, smoothing it with your hand as you do so.

PROJECTS

Sit at the height which is most comfortable for you to work at. Your bundle of damp rushes should be close at hand.

SECTION THREE

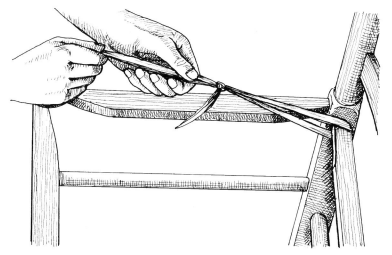

Looping the first length of rush before commencing a new seat.

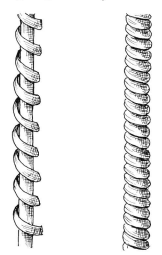

Rush should be coiled tightly (above right) and not loosely (above left).

2 Loop this twisted strand underneath the chair on to the left-hand rail. Move on to the front rail and so on until you have gone round in a square. Then pass over and under the right-hand rail.

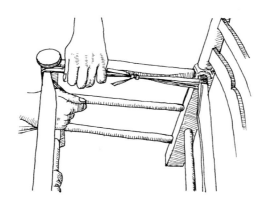

PROJECTS

Twisting the lengths of rush to make a single coil.

Beginning to wrap the rush around the frame.

3 Continue round, filling in the corners and adding new rushes as necessary by twisting as described before, but always maintaining the same twisted thickness so that the final effect is even. Should you need

to join a rush at a corner, the neatest way to do so is to lift the working rush before forming the right angle, and tuck the butt end of the new one underneath it so that an end of about 5 cm/2 inches hangs downwards. Twist the old and new rushes together to form the new, working strand and as this passes under the seat, bring it under the protruding butt end to hide it and keep the underside neat. Eventually, the whole seat will be filled; if there is still a hole in the middle where the side rails are often shorter, work the rush backwards and forwards until it is completed.

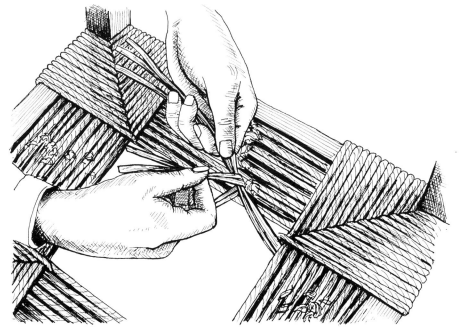

Joining a fresh length of rush.

4 Turning the seat upside down, tuck your last piece of rush between the top and bottom layers of the work using your stuffing stick – a rushworker's wooden implement useful for exactly this purpose. While you are working on the underside, trim off any ends to neaten.

PROJECTS

*Gradually the frame fills towards the centre. If there is still a hole,
work the rush backwards and forwards until it is filled.*

The rushwork seat should be kept as neatly finished on the underside as it is on top.

5 The final stage is to poke any scraps of rush and cut off the ends between the top and bottom layers of your rushwork with your stuffing stick. This pads out the seat and makes it more comfortable; it also helps to stop it sinking or sagging.

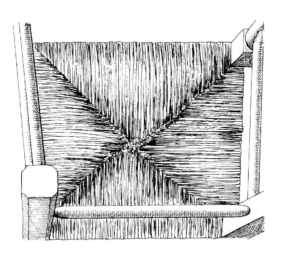

*Tidying up any loose ends and pushing them inside
with the stuffing stick.*

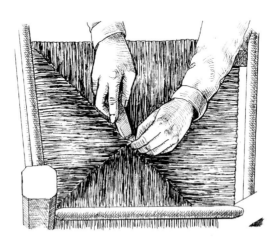

*A rush-seated chair is padded with small rush offcuts by pushing
them between the layers from underneath.*

SECTION THREE

PROJECT SIX

◆ LARGE CIRCULAR LOG BASKET ◆

Round baskets are the easiest to make and are ideal for beginners; the more experienced basket-maker might experiment with more elaborate weave patterns and shape variations such as a bowl or waisted design; or move on to square work such as bottle baskets and hampers which require the aid of a special block to make the base. Once you have mastered the round basket process, you could adapt this not just to the large log basket shown here, but also, for example, to a shopper with a single handle, a low-sided fruit basket, a cheese tray or wastepaper-basket. The possibilities are endless using just the few basic steps.

Using different coloured willows such as whites and buffs, or dyed canes, adds further possibilities in colour patterns and designs. Baskets can be worked in cane, willow or any flexible stem material although the latter is less manageable and harder to handle. Willow base sticks with cane weavers is a popular combination for beginners. Willow should be pre-soaked until pliable (page 34).

Work sitting on the floor or at a table of a comfortable height with your selected material close at hand: a pile of osier rods disappears quicker than you think and jumping up and down to replenish supplies is not just a nuisance, it breaks your concentration too.

1 You begin by making the base of the basket which is called a slath. You need your thickest, stoutest rods for this, probably cut from the butt end and as even in thickness as you can make them. The length of these will determine the eventual size of your basket, so bear this in mind when making your selection. They can be cut smaller but not made bigger.

Half the sticks are carefully pierced with a sharp knife to make a slit, then the other sticks are pushed carefully through at right angles. This is quite tricky as it has to be done without splitting the stick in half. A convenient sized bodkin is useful for widening the split sufficiently to

66

push the stick through. Since the sticks will naturally taper slightly, arrange them alternately butt, tip, butt, tip, to avoid the slath looking uneven. Generally four sticks run each way in a slath.

Classic log basket, squarework bottle carrier and a tiny decorative basket – the rattles which contain small bells were taken from a traditional design intended to finish off the legs of wickerwork chairs.

SECTION THREE

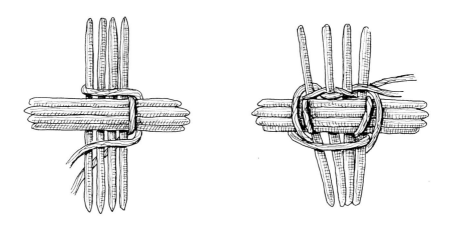

Binding the slath.

2 Using the method known as pairing, these sticks are bound together with a long but much thinner piece of material, called a weaver. A single long weaver is looped around one arm of the stick cross you have made (the slath), then twisted left over right, to pass the ends on either side of the arm lying immediately clockwise (right). The slath is turned in the hands 90° anticlockwise (left) and the process repeated.

When you have been right round a couple of times and the cross is well bound, pull the sticks apart firmly to make the spokes of a wheel. Adjust them in pairs first, then singly. It is important that these spokes are evenly spaced. As you pull each one apart, the weaver follows: take it down behind the next stick and hold it there while you adjust the space, then bring it through the front so that it goes over and under, holding the sticks in place.

It is important to pull the weavers as tight as possible; otherwise the basket will look very loosely woven and probably uneven when it dries. To join weavers as work progresses, tips (the thin ends) should be matched to tips and butts to butts so there is no ugly change of thickness.

PROJECTS

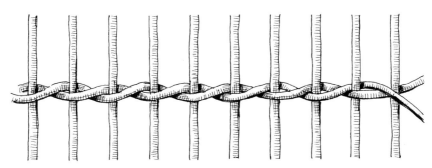

Pairing technique.

3 As the weaving around the base takes shape, 'pairing' in and out around the spokes, you should be coaxing the base into a slightly convex shape – like a shallow upside-down dish. This whole process can be skipped if you use a wooden base. These are supplied complete with holes to take the side stakes (pages 26–7). However, a wooden base produces a totally different-looking item; it is sometimes ideally suited to a canework tray or pot stand. Instructions for preparing wooden bases are given on page 28.

4 When the base has reached the size you want, the upright stakes are inserted. Normally these are placed on either side of a base stick (your spokes). First cut the spokes around the base to the required length and trim away any protruding ends of weavers. The upright stakes need to be tall enough to cover the height of the basket and the edging, and must be pointed so that they can be easily inserted in the base. This is called 'slyping' and involves making a point in the end with a sharp knife.

The butt end is slyped, then pushed about 5 cm/2 inches into the weave of the base all round, so that it looks like a giant wheel – at this stage you will realize why you need plenty of space around you when basket-making! Each stake is then kinked with a knife in the appropriate place so that it can be bent upwards to form the upright stakes without cracking or breaking.

SECTION THREE

For some weave patterns an uneven number of stakes is required, in which case the odd one is inserted down the side of another, then spaced out evenly. A hoop or length of twine is fitted around the top of the raised stakes to help to keep them in place while you weave the sides.

5 You then work the bottom rim of the basket which must be strong and stable. Choosing rods roughly the same thickness as your upright stakes, slype the butt end and push into the base close by the stakes. The weaving process is called 'waling' and can be done with three, four, five or six rods – a four-rod wale is a manageable size for a beginner. The process works round the base from left to right, weaving each rod in turn, in front of two stakes and then behind two. Make sure your work is taut and firm.

It is important that the first complete row lies as tight and close as possible, so press the cane or willow down firmly into place with a metal file or basket-maker's beater. Then work the second round, deciding what shape the final basket will be by adjusting the upright spokes – if you allow them to splay out, you will get a very open-necked basket. Most baskets have three rows of waling.

6 The rest of the basket is completed using one or more of a variety of weaving techniques. Pairing as for the base is one option; variations of 'randing' and 'slewing' offer many more. Basic randing involves weaving single rods of a similar length in and out between an even number of stakes.

Start by laying the butt end of a rod between two stakes from the inside, and weave it in and out until you have been all the way round once. The second weaver is inserted butt-end between the next two stakes to the right and woven round as before. You can carry on in this manner for as long as you like, providing you make sure the butts lie to the inside of the basket and the tips to the outside; these are trimmed off at a later stage.

7 In French randing, the butt of a weaving rod is laid in and worked just one rand; a second of the same length and thickness is then inserted to the left of the first and this is also worked one rand. New rods are inserted and worked all the way round. Each to the left is then worked one stroke at a time until they are all played out. This can be done over any number of stakes.

Rib randing, on the other hand, takes the weaving rod in front of two stakes and then behind one to create a different pattern. This can only be done where the number of stakes is not divisible by three.

8 Slewing works over an uneven number of stakes using two or more weavers at a time. You start with a single weaver as in randing, but when this has been worked for about half its length, a second weaver is introduced just ahead of it. The two are then worked together as a pair; when one runs out, the tip is left on the outside and another new rod inserted just ahead of the second rod as before to keep the pair. You can also work a slew with three rods.

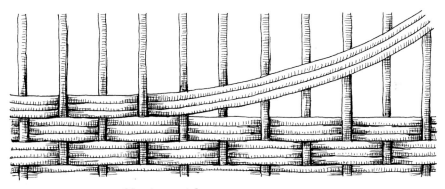

Slewing with two or more canes.

9 When your basket has almost reached its required height, you should decide what kind of border you want to give it along the top edge. It must be strong and practical but many of the border designs are attractive too. Finish your weaving with a couple of rows of waling

to match the base (see above) to help firm up the top and keep its shape. Your border is made with the length of remaining upright stakes. By this time, they will have become rather dry so wet them first with a hand spray or soak with a damp sponge until they are suitably pliable – or you run the risk of their cracking and spoiling the finish of your basket.

A plain basket border.

10 Again there are various options based on two basic techniques: trac (track) and plain borders. A simple trac border bends over each stake in turn – again you may need to coax it with your metal bar or file to lie flat. It is then taken behind the neighbouring rod to the right and in front of the next two, to the left behind the next. Plain borders simply follow the 'behind one' or 'behind two' routine, working with two, three, four, five or six rods.

Trac border with double stakes suitable for a shopping basket.

PROJECTS

11 If you want your basket to have some kind of handle, again the choice is wide. A strong wrapped handle – such as on a shopping basket – is made by slyping and inserting two canes or rods of the same length about 2.5 cm/1 inch apart on each side of the basket, with a third midway between each pair. Measure the top of the basket carefully to get the positions equal.

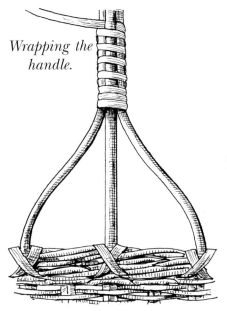

Wrapping the handle.

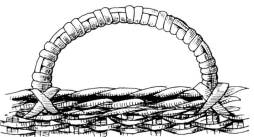

Front view of a small wrapped handle.

Draw the two handles together at the top, overlapping by about 13–15 cm/5–6 inches, and secure with 1 cm/$\frac{1}{2}$ inch thin wire nails. Make a hole through the base of each rod or cane and thread a thin rod or piece of wrapping cane through it, securing the short end in the weaving. Thread the long end over the border to secure the rod with a cross, then secure one side in the border and continue the other right the way over to wrap the handle.

Insert two thinner rods or lengths of cane in front of the central rod and use the weaver to wrap these together about four times at the base before passing twice under and over alternately. The ends are finally secured in the border at the other end with a cross as before. The last end is then threaded sideways into the weave, passing it in front of and behind a few stakes, to fasten. Finish on the inside of the basket and trim off any straggly ends.

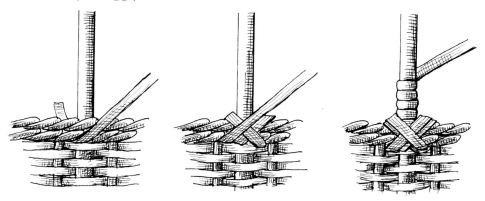

Wrapping the base of a handle. From left to right, inserting the cane, crossing it and wrapping the handle.

12 To make small wrapped side handles, as on a log or workbasket, bend a largish rod or cane with slyped ends over into the border and thread down the side of the basket to secure. Position two smaller rods on either side and with lighter weaving rods or canes, secure with a cross as before (see above) and continue to wrap the handle, moving over and under the rods as described earlier. Finish with a securing cross in front of the border as described for the single wrapped style. Repeat the whole procedure on the other side for matching handles.

Tall laundry basket specially commissioned for the cloakrooms at the House of Lords in London. It is a perfect example of basketwork's flexible nature and its functional quality.

PROJECTS

PROJECT SEVEN

◆ BASKET REPAIRS ◆

Attractive old cane and willow baskets are surprisingly sturdy but if a particular favourite or a junk shop bargain is damaged, it is sometimes possible to effect a convincing repair. The most difficult aspect is matching the colour and finish but this can often be faked using stains and dyes to imitate the mellowing of time and wear.

Another problem may be acquiring materials in such small quantities: if you do not wish to make new baskets as well as repair an old one, contact a basket-maker or craft group near you through the appropriate national association or guild and ask if they will let you have just the pieces you need.

REPAIRING THE SIDE WEAVING ON A CANE OR WILLOW BASKET

As well as soaking your material where necessary, the basket must also be soaked for several hours to make it more pliable. Remove the broken parts and weave in new rods or canes to match, tucking the ends into the existing weave and then trimming. A small bodkin may be useful for 'losing' the ends in the existing weaving. Remember to match butts to tips, not butts to butts.

REPAIRING UPRIGHT STAKES

If an upright stake has broken, it may be possible to pull out the broken pieces and thread a new one down the side by slyping a piece of rod or cane (No. 6) and using a bodkin to push it well down into the weave. Kink the new stake level with the top of the border and thread the tip into the border following the existing pattern and using the bodkin to make way for it between the weave.

With wooden bases where the upright stakes are damaged, the base weaving has sometimes been damaged or unravelled too. To repair this, you will need to insert new stakes up through the holes in the bottom of the base, allowing them to extend a few cm/inches into the

76

PROJECTS

weave. Reweave the waling at the base. If, however, too many of the upright stakes are repaired in this way, the basket will be very weak.

REPAIRING RUSH BASKETS

This is fairly easily done providing the rushes are pre-soaked as described on page 35 – they should match the original as closely as possible. It is not usually necessary to soak the basket too.

A broken stake can be repaired by threading a thick rush into the weave so that it overlaps the break by several rows. The ends are trimmed at an angle when dry. If the border is damaged, the broken stakes should be replaced by threading a thinner rush into the weave, overlapping the break slightly on each side of the damage.

Repairing a broken weaver by threading a thinner rush into the weave, overlapping the break by about 2.5 cm/1 inch on each side of the break.

SECTION THREE

Rush baskets usually have soft handles made of twisted rush. If one of these is damaged, remove it completely and weave an even number of rushes (arranged with the butts and tips alternating to even out the width) through the original hole in the side of the basket to several rows down the weave. Pull them half-way through and twist each half to the right until they meet above the border. Lay the right-hand coil over the left one and twist to the right before laying over the left. Keeping twisting the right hand, pass one turn to the right, then lay it over the rushes on the left hand to form a new rope.

When the handle is the desired length, bring the ends of the two coils to the opposite side of the basket. Thread one coil to the outside, inserting them both into the hole of the original handle. Thread the ends of each strand into the weave, following the pattern as closely as possible passing one to the right and one to the left of the handle. Weave in and out a few times, finish on the inside, trim and neaten.

REPAIRING A CANE OR WILLOW BASKET HANDLE

You can buy ready-bowed wooden handles for baskets or you can make these yourself using handle cane, thick willow rod or an even piece of ash or hazel. Measure the old handle and cut the new one to fit allowing at least 10 cm/4 inches on each side for inserting into the side of the basket. Slype each end of the new piece and make a channel to slip it into using an appropriately sized bodkin.

Soak both the basket and the new handle until they are more workable, then try to push the new handle into place, matching the angle of the old handle as closely as possible. Push the ends as far down as possible into the weave of the basket, then cover the handle by winding with osiers or wrapping with glossy lapping cane, securing with a cross at both ends as described above.

Secure the handle with a peg of willow or cane driven into a small hole – leave it protruding slightly so that it rests against the weave of the basket; alternatively tap a small tack right through the main basket into the handle with a hammer.

SECTION FOUR

*T*IPS AND

*S*HORT *C*UTS

*W*hether under the guidance of a master craftsperson or just following the instructions in a book, it is always worth knowing a few tips on how to avoid known pitfalls or how to make a job a little quicker or easier.

◆ CANING ◆

QUICK SETTING FOR CANING

For speed when caning a large number of chairs, the professionals use a 'steamer'. Double a piece of cane by folding it in half, then weave it in and out one way. Tuck another piece of doubled cane into the loop you made by folding it, then pull backwards and forwards like a shuttle. It means you can just pull it through instead of laboriously weaving in and out: a very quick way to do setting providing you don't forget the point you have reached.

HOLDING ON

Every beginner is taught to keep hold of one end of the cane. It prevents your losing it and means you are not forever picking it up – after a while keeping the end in one hand becomes automatic.

SECTION FOUR

TWISTING AND TURNING

The right side of your seating-cane should be the glossy side, so do ensure the cane is kept the same way up throughout the job. Also watch out for the cane twisting in the holes or underneath the seat and check regularly that the cane is not crossed or twisted when working settings. Try to keep the finish as neat as possible both on top and underneath the seat.

CHECKING KNOTS

Check your knots to ensure that they are tight enough and that they cannot get pulled up into the holes.

THE RIGHT SIZE PEGS

Pegs should be thick enough not to allow them to be pressed in with the fingers, but not in so tight that they split when you tap them in with a hammer.

SHEET CANING

You will find many modern cane chairs feature seats and/or backs made from a pre-woven cane called sheet cane finished with a beading strip of round (or pulp) cane. The sheet is glued into a groove that runs around the perimeter of the chair frame and is not nearly as robust as a traditionally caned chair.

Begin by cutting away all the old cane with a knife, and scrape away any remains of glue or cane from the groove. Soak the new sheet in cold water for around 15 minutes. Woodworking adhesive can then be run all the way round the relevant groove, making sure that both the sides and bottom are covered; use a small stick to press the glue right into the groove if necessary.

The sheet can then be laid in the appropriate place, ensuring that the lines of caning are parallel to the straight side of the chair. Use a hammer to tap a wedge into the groove at the centre back of the chair, forcing the sheet of cane into the groove. By smoothing and stretching

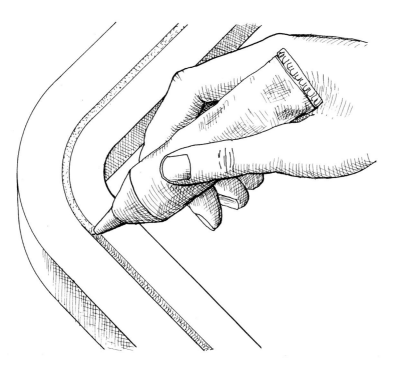

Run woodworking adhesive into the groove.

the damp cane down and across, a second wedge can be tapped in at the front, and then two more in the middle on either side. Making sure the cane remains parallel to the sides of the frame, further wedges are inserted in pairs on opposite sides of the chair. A spare wedge can then be used to tap all round with the hammer inserting every bit of sheet into the groove; you will need to take special care at the corners. The wedge should prevent the hammer from damaging the cane, provided that you do not tap it too roughly. Do not stretch the damp cane sheet too much or it may not fit snugly enough once it has dried. Ideally there should be a small amount overlapping which can be trimmed at a later stage (see page 83).

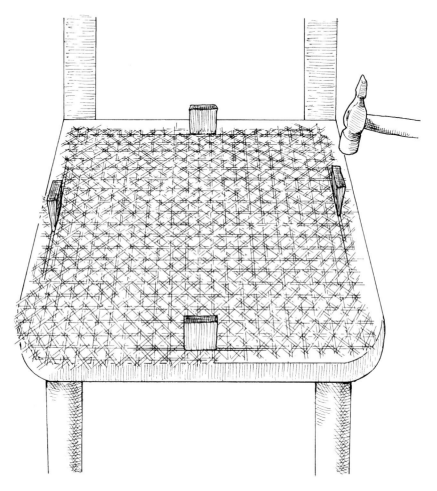

Tap wedges into the groove to force the panel down on to the frame.

The wedges can then be removed and the sheet left for the glue to set. Meanwhile, run the glue into the groove on top of the cane and cut a piece of finishing (round) cane to the required length. This can be tapped into the groove using the hammer and the thick end of one of the wedges. It should be level with the seat. If the chair seat or back has a curve, you will have to cut sections of cane to fit.

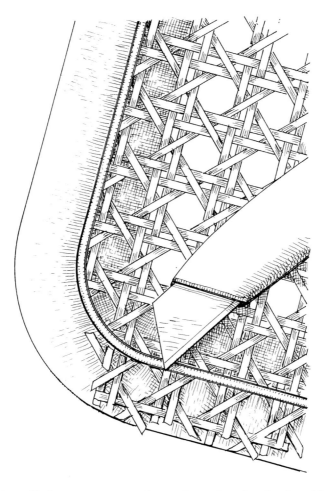

*Trim off the excess cane sheet when the glue is dry. Note
the cane border in place.*

When the glue has dried, you can trim away the surplus sheet cane
with a sharp knife, taking care not to leave any sharp edges sticking
out. This is most easily done by pointing the blade of the knife against
the outside edge of the groove, while resting the flat of the blade on
the finishing cane.

◆ RUSH ◆

DAMAGED RUSHES

Always discard any rushes that crack or split while being worked as they will weaken the whole seat when finished. Since you are effectively working with a single piece of material on a square frame, a single flaw could ruin the whole project.

KEEPING IT SQUARE

Check your work periodically to ensure that it stays square: the rush should fit snugly where it crosses and not overlap its neighbour.

MAINTAINING TENSION

The work should be kept as taut as possible and checked to ensure that one piece does not ride over another, especially on the underside of the seat. Each time you go round the chair, the rush should be pushed tightly against the previous one on each rail.

MAKING A CORD OR ROPE

To make a cord or rope, the strands are not simply twisted together, but are wound together into a single rope. This is done by moulding the cord into shape with one hand and twisting with the other.

◆ BASKET-MAKING ◆

WEAVING AN EVEN STAKED BASKET

To avoid any overlap by stopping and starting your weaving at the same point, move the basket a quarter turn after each row. This way you won't have to search for the end on the last row and will know directly where to begin the next.

TIPS AND SHORT CUTS

PERFECTING THE SHAPE

To maintain a good symmetrical shape, keep checking your work – from a slight distance if necessary. If it needs adjusting, wet with a plant sprayer – taking care not to wet any wooden base or hoops – and manipulate with your hands until you have corrected any irregularities. This must be done as the work progresses as you will not be able to reshape the basket after it is finished.

REPLACING A BROKEN STAKE

If a stake breaks or is too short, it can be repaired by cutting a piece similar in size and sliding it into the weaving on top of the broken stake down to the base of the basket. Expose the new piece to the outside of the basket.

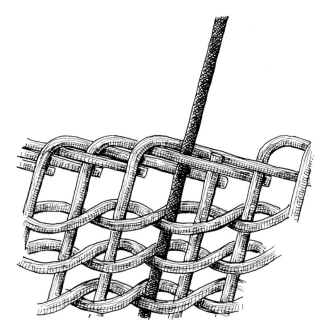

Make a space with a bodkin, then push the new stake well down into the weave.

SECTION FOUR

NON-WOVEN BASKETS

An attractive but not particularly sturdy country style basket can be made by tying short bundles of clipped material and fixing them into the holes of a ready-made wooden base – you sometimes see such baskets in florists and gift shops. However, this type of basket can only be used for display or ornamental purposes.

DIRECTION OF WILLOW

Willow should always be worked with the thicker butt end lying to the inside and the tips to the outside. Always leave trimming the ends until the basket is finished, then simply go round and tidy it up, taking care to cut the ends at an angle so that they lie snugly, and not too close to the basket or they will slip through the weaving and unravel as it dries and shrinks.

GLOSSARY

Ash splint: strip of ash thinned enough to use as a stake or weaver in basket making.

Awl: tool used for opening spaces between weaving or to tuck in ends.

Base: the bottom of a basket or tray.

Beading: round shaped cane running around the edge to conceal the threading holes.

Bevel: to cut a square edge to a sloping edge.

Bodkins: different sized screwdriver-like tools for opening spaces in weaving.

Bolt: bundles in which rush is purchased.

Border: top edge of a basket.

Brake: a short piece of reed woven alternately above the beginning of a weaver to hold it in place.

Butt: the thicker end of an osier; to bring two ends flush against each other.

GLOSSARY

Chase weave: method of weaving with two weavers simultaneously.

Coil: weaving technique which works from an inner core and winds about itself, working outwards.

Continuous weave: weaving done over an odd number of stakes. Instead of one row at a time, the weavers are added periodically and worked continuously from beginning to end.

Couching: cane used to hold beading in place.

Crossings: canes running diagonally across the panel; and woven through the settings.

D handle: basket handle that continues across the bottom of the basket and so resembles the letter 'd' when on its side.

Diagonal weave: method of weaving where the elements interweave themselves. Sometimes called oblique weaving or diagonal plaiting.

Double bottom: basket technique whereby a second woven base is placed on top of the first.

Doubling: caning technique working from top to bottom.

French randing: basketweave method whereby a series of rods is worked in turn.

Lasher: piece of reed used on some baskets to wrap around and secure all the rim pieces.

Osier: willow.

GLOSSARY

Pairing: basketwork method where two or more elements are twisted around each other as they weave around the stakes. Sometimes called 'twining'.

Rand: an over-and-under basket-making technique using single weavers of similar length and an even number of stakes.

Settings: canes which run from front to back and side to side in the basic weaving pattern.

Slath: interlaced sticks used as the base for baskets.

Slewing: two or more paired weavers worked in a randing pattern over an uneven number of stakes.

Slype: the slanting cut made at the end of a willow so that it can be easily inserted.

Stake: parts of the woven base which are upsett to create the upright elements.

Stuffing stick: tool used to stuff a rush seat with spare rush for padding.

Three-rod wale: basketweaving technique where three weavers are inserted, each behind three consecutive stakes and moving over two, then under one.

Tip: thin end of a rod or reed.

Tucking in: where the outside stakes of a basket are pointed, bent over and tucked into the weaving on the inside of the basket. Sometimes called 'down staking'.

GLOSSARY

Upsetting: to bend the stakes up and over upon themselves to create the crease at the base of the stake when basket-making.

Waling: basketweaving technique using three, four, five or six rods.

Web: the interwoven lattice of canes making up a seat or back panel.

_I_NDEX

Page numbers in italic refer to illustrations

INDEX

INDEX

INDEX

INDEX